No-Fuss 5-Minute Meal

Recipes

Heartwarming Meals That Are Ready in A Jiffy

by Will C.

Copyright Page

Table of Contents

Introduction

Cooking should always be a fun thing and never a pain.

With advanced technology for food prep, cooking has become one of the easiest things. A little combination of quick-cooking ingredients gets the job done.

In this cookbook, we explore using quick-cooking ingredients and leftovers to create sumptuous meals that you wouldn't believe could be done in 5 minutes or under.

There are options for breakfast, lunch, dinner, dessert, and snacks to create delightful cooking moments for you.

Scan through the options that we offer and as always, be at ease to tweak the ingredients to fit your needs. Just ensure that they'll offer quick-cooking results like the recipes.

Are you ready to explore the 5-minute meals that we have for you?

Come along!

Chocolate Strawberry Mug Cake

Chocolate and strawberry cake is almost everyone's favorite but we often do not have nearly an hour to bake a full-blown cake. This microwave mug cake is your easy route to enjoying this cake as quickly as you want.

Serves: 1

Ready Time: 45 seconds

Ingredients:

- ¼ tsp baking powder
- 1 tbsp all-purpose flour
- 1 tsp cocoa powder
- 2 tsp granulated sugar
- A small pinch of salt
- 1 to 1-½ tbsp hot water or a little more to thin
- 2 tsp vegetable oil
- ¼ tsp white vinegar
- 1 tbsp strawberry jam
- ¼ tsp vanilla extract
- 1 or 2 strawberries for garnish

Instructions:

1. In a bowl, combine flour, baking powder, cocoa powder, sugar, and salt. Mix well.

2. Add remaining ingredients and whisk until smooth batter forms.

3. Pour mixture into a mug and microwave on high for 30 to 45 seconds or until cake sets in the center.

4. Remove cake and let cool.

5. Garnish with strawberries and serve.

Quick Omelette

Omelette makes breakfast shine. While it cooks quickly in a skillet, this ramekin microwave version makes it faster. And it tastes just as good.

Serves: 4

Ready Time: 3 mins

Ingredients:

- 2 eggs
- ½ small green bell pepper, deseeded and chopped
- 1 small tomato, chopped
- 2 slices ham, diced
- Salt and pepper to taste

Instructions

1. Crack eggs into a ramekin and lightly beat.

2. Add remaining ingredients and mix well.

3. Microwave on high for 2 to 3 minutes or until eggs set at center.

4. Remove ramekin from microwave, let cool slightly and enjoy.

Quick Leftover Tacos

All you need to do here is warm your tortillas in the broiler for 1 to 2 minutes and load it with some leftovers. Voila!

Serves: 4

Ready Time: 5 mins

Ingredients:

- 8 mini tortillas
- 1 cup leftover cooked meat (chicken, beef, etc.)
- 1 cup salsa
- ½ small red onion, thinly sliced
- Fresh cilantro leaves for garnish
- Hot sauce for topping

Instructions:

1. Warm tortillas in a broiler for 1 to 2 minutes.

2. Remove onto a clean flat surface and divide remaining ingredients on top.

3. Serve.

Simple Mozzarella Sticks

Don't fret over making mozzarella sticks. The deep fryer set on high heat cooks it quickly. Also, use pre-seasoned breadcrumbs or crushed cornflakes to shorten your coating time.

Serves: 4

Ready Time: 3 mins

Ingredients:

- Oil for frying
- 1 cup mozzarella sticks, cut to your preferred length
- 1 egg, lightly beaten
- 1 cup seasoned Panko breadcrumbs or crushed cornflakes
- Salsa or marinara sauce for serving

Instructions:

1. Heat oil in a deep fryer on high heat.

2. Dip each mozzarella sticks in egg and then coat well in breadcrumbs.

3. Fry in oil for 2 to 3 minutes or until golden brown.

4. Transfer to a paper towel-lined plate to drain grease.

5. Serve with salsa or marinara sauce.

Microwave Raspberry Cheesecake

We love cheesecake so much and we hope you do too. Here's the fun part, you can make it in under 5 minutes. Want to know how? Check out our trick below.

Serves: 1

Ready Time: 5 mins

Ingredients:

- 1 tbsp butter
- 2 graham crackers, crushed
- 4 oz cream cheese, softened
- 2 tbsp granulated sugar
- ½ tsp vanilla extract
- 5 fresh raspberries for serving

Instructions:

1. In a bowl, combine graham crackers and butter. Mix well and add to a small ramekin. Use a teaspoon to press crust to bottom of ramekin.

2. In another bowl, whisk cream cheese, sugar, and vanilla until smooth. Add mixture to ramekin and spread evenly.

3. Microwave cheesecake for 4 to 5 minutes with 45 seconds power intervals while making sure cream cheese doesn't rise and pour over ramekin.

4. Remove cheesecake and let chill in refrigerator until ready to enjoy.

Filling Smoothie

Assembling breakfast is faster than you think. Gather some fruits, nuts, seeds, yogurt, milk, etc. and blend them up into a tasty smoothie. This recipe offers a filling one.

Serves: 1

Ready Time: 2 mins

Ingredients:

- 1 cup frozen strawberries or fruit of choice
- ¼ cup plain Greek yogurt
- 1 tbsp nut butter of choice
- 2 tsp honey or maple syrup
- 1 tsp vanilla extract
- ¾ cup milk of choice
- Nuts or granola for topping

Instructions:

1. Add all ingredients to a blender and process until smooth.

2. Pour into a glass, add toppings and enjoy.

Barbecue Chicken Nachos

Nachos are some of the tastiest snacks. Load up your nachos with your favorites and microwave for a few minutes. There you have a cheesy, juicy bunch.

Serves: 1

Ready Time: 3 mins

Ingredients:

- 1 to 1 ½ cups tortilla chips
- 1 cup shredded rotisserie chicken
- 3 tbsp BBQ sauce
- ¼ cup pico de gallo
- 1 cup grated cheddar cheese
- ¼ cup thinly sliced red onion
- Sour cream for topping
- Chopped fresh cilantro for garnish
- Guacamole to serve

Instructions:

1. Spread tortilla chips on a plate.

2. Combine chicken with BBQ sauce and spread on tortilla chips.

3. Spread pico de gallo on top, then cheddar cheese, and green onion.

4. Microwave for 1 to 3 minutes or until cheese melts.

5. Remove from oven, top with sour cream and garnish with cilantro.

6. Serve with guacamole.

Mac "n" Cheese

It sounds unbelievable until you try it. Mac and cheese in a mug is such a delight. It is a quick treat that doesn't require many minutes of cooking and baking to make.

Serves: 1

Ready Time: 4 mins

Ingredients:

- ¼ cup grated cheddar cheese
- ½ cup elbow macaroni
- Salt and black pepper to taste
- 3 tbsp milk of choice
- ½ cup water
- Chopped fresh scallions for garnish

Instructions:

1. Combine macaroni, water, and salt in a mug. Stir and microwave for 2 to 3 minutes.

2. Add milk, cheddar cheese, and black pepper. Stir and microwave for 30 seconds to 1 minute.

3. Remove from microwave, stir and garnish with scallions.

4. Serve warm.

5-Minute Pizza

And just like that, pizza is ready for you in 3 minutes. Unbelievable! With a little trick, using a tortilla as the crust, you can enjoy pizza as quickly and often as you want.

Serves: 1

Ready Time: 3 mins

Ingredients:

- 1 large tortilla
- 2 tbsp pizza sauce
- ¼ tsp dried basil
- ¼ cup grated mozzarella cheese
- ¼ cup pepperoni slices

Instructions:

1. Lay tortilla on a plate and spread pizza sauce on top.

2. Spread basil on top, then mozzarella cheese, and pepperoni.

3. Broil for 3 minutes or until cheese melts.

4. Remove from oven and let cool slightly before serving.

Chicken Quesadillas

This no-fret chicken quesadillas is an excellent breakfast treat. It uses leftover chicken for quicker cooking time.

Serves: 1

Ready Time: 3 mins

Ingredients:

- 1 large tortilla
- ⅓ cup grated meltable cheese of choice
- ¼ cup shredded rotisserie chicken
- ¼ cup chopped bell pepper
- 2 tbsp canned corn
- Salsa for topping

Instructions:

1. Heat a skillet over medium heat.

2. Place tortilla in skillet and on one half side, spread chicken, bell pepper, corn, and salsa. On other half, spread cheese and let melt.

3. Lift cheese side onto chicken side and cook for 1 more minute.

4. Transfer to a plate and slice into wedges. Serve.

Burrito Bowl

Gather your favorite burrito fillings in a bowl, warm them in the microwave and enjoy. That simple!

Serves: 1

Ready Time: 2 mins

Ingredients:

- 1 cup cooked brown rice
- ½ cup canned black beans, drained and rinsed
- 1 tbsp plain Greek yogurt
- 2 to 3 tbsp salsa or to taste
- 1 tbsp shredded cheddar cheese
- Toppings:
- Diced tomato
- Diced avocado
- Guacamole
- Pico de gallo

Instructions

1. Combine all ingredients in a bowl except for toppings. Microwave for 30 to 60 seconds or until warmed through.

2. Remove from microwave and add toppings.

3. Serve.

Veggie Sushi Bowl

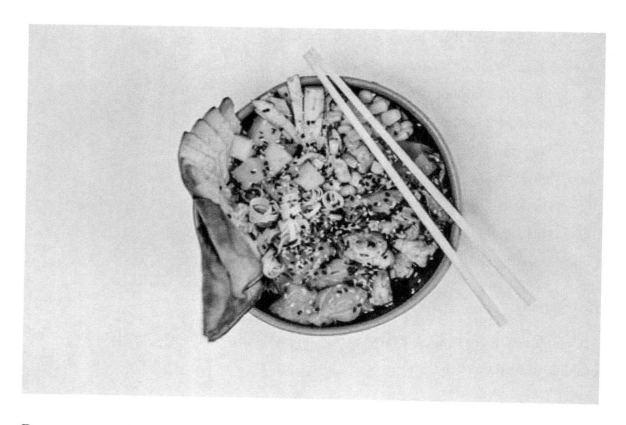

Deconstruct sushi into this bowl of yummy goodness. With pre-cooked sushi rice, everything else becomes an easy assemble. Gathering the ingredients in a bowl other than rolling them up into sushi, shortens the time a great deal.

Serves: 1

Ready Time: 3 mins

Ingredients:

Dressing:

- ½ tbsp sesame oil
- ½ tbsp white vinegar
- 1 tsp honey
- 1 tbsp soy sauce

Sushi bowl:

- ½ cup sushi rice, cooked
- 1 avocado, pitted, peeled, and chopped
- ½ mango, chopped
- A handful of micro greens
- ¼ cup sliced radish
- ½ cup grated red cabbage
- 1 tsp black sesame seeds for garnish

Instructions:

1. In a bowl, combine all dressing ingredients and whisk well.

2. Add sushi rice to bottom of a bowl and add remaining toppings.

3. Drizzle some dressing on top and garnish with sesame seeds.

4. Serve.

Grilled Cheese

Grilled cheese is such a pampering treat, which gets ready in little time. Enjoy!

Serves: 1

Ready Time: 4 mins

Ingredients:

- 2 bread slices
- 1 tbsp melted butter
- ½ cup grated cheddar cheese

Instructions:

1. Heat a grill pan, skillet, or toaster over medium heat.

2. Brush bread slices on both sides with butter.

3. On one bread slice, load cheese and cover with other bread slice.

4. Grill in skillet for 1 to 2 minutes per side or until cheese melts and bread is golden brown. Serve.

Tasty Hummus

Hummus is an excellent and filling snack that pairs well with pita chips, biscuits, crackers, and veggies. It is ready in 2 minutes.

Serves: 4

Ready Time: 2 mins

Ingredients:

- 2 (15 oz) canned chickpeas, drained (about ⅓ cup of liquid reserved for thinning)
- ½ cup tahini
- ¼ cup olive oil
- 2 lemons, juiced
- 2 garlic cloves
- 1 tsp cumin powder
- Salt to taste

Garnish:

- Olive oil
- Paprika
- Chopped fresh parsley

Instructions:

1. Add all ingredients to a food processor except for garnishing ones. Blend until smooth.

2. Pour hummus into a bowl and garnish with olive oil, paprika, and parsley.

3. Serve with pita chips, veggies, etc.

Quinoa Salad

Grab some leftover quinoa, add some nutritious elements like pomegranate arils, vegetables, herbs, nuts, and seeds for a super healthy salad.

Serves: 1

Ready Time: 2 mins

Ingredients:

Dressing:

- ¼ cup pomegranate juice
- 1 lemon, zested and juiced
- ¼ to ½ cup extra virgin olive oil
- Salt and black pepper to taste

Salad:

- 2 cups pre-cooked quinoa
- ¼ cup pomegranate arils
- ⅓ cup dried cranberries
- ⅓ cup sliced green onion
- ⅓ cup nuts and seeds of choice
- ⅓ cup roughly chopped fresh parsley

Instructions:

1. Combine all of the dressing ingredients in a bowl and whisk well.

2. Add all salad ingredients to another bowl and mix well.

3. Drizzle some dressing on top and toss well.

4. Add more dressing if needed and serve.

Peanut Butter, Banana, and Blueberry Toast

This filling breakfast looks like a project but is super easy to make and extremely delicious.

Serves: 1

Ready Time: 2 mins

Ingredients:

- 2 bread slices
- 2 tbsp peanut butter, smooth and creamy
- 1 fresh banana, peeled and sliced
- A handful of fresh blueberries
- Toasted peanuts for garnish

Instructions:

1. Toast bread in a skillet or toaster.

2. Spread peanut butter on one side of each bread slice.

3. Top with banana, blueberries, and peanuts. Serve.

Apple and Feta Flatbread

A delicious flatbread treat to love. Explore different quick-cooking toppings for variety.

Serves: 1

Ready Time: 3 mins

Ingredients:

- 1 large flatbread
- ½ cup cranberry or cherry jam
- 1 apple, cored and cut into ½-inch cubes
- ½ cup crumbled feta cheese
- ¼ cup chopped nuts of choice

Instructions

1. Lay flatbread on a baking sheet and spread cranberry or cherry jam on top.

2. Add apple, feta cheese, and nuts.

3. Broil in oven for 2 to 3 minutes or until cheese melts.

Chicken and Blue Cheese Lettuce Cups

You can serve these salad cups for appetizers or have them for lunch. Either way, they are flavor-packed and delicious with a nice crunch.

Serves: 1

Ready Time: 3 mins

Ingredients:

- ⅓ to ½ cup crumbled blue cheese
- ¼ cup Greek yogurt
- ½ lemon, juiced
- 1 cup shredded rotisserie chicken
- 8 large romaine lettuce leaves, sturdy pieces
- 2 to 3 tbsp chopped toasted walnuts
- 8 berries of choice, halved
- 2 tsp chopped fresh chives

Instructions:

1. In a bowl, combine blue cheese, Greek yogurt, and lemon juice. Mix well not necessarily smooth but well-distributed.

2. Add chicken and toss well.

3. Lay lettuce leaves on a clean, flat surface and fill with chicken mixture. Top with walnuts, berries, and chives.

Mason Jar Ramen

Don't fret over making ramen. This lunch recipe is perfect to assemble and enjoy when the kids are back from school.

Serves: 1

Ready Time: 3 mins

Ingredients:

- 1 tsp bouillon paste
- 3 tbsp hot sauce
- ½ cup chopped or shredded vegetables of choice (carrots, cabbage, bell peppers, spinach, etc.)
- 1 cup cooked brown rice noodles
- 1 tbsp sliced scallions

Instructions:

1. Add bouillon paste to bottom of a mason jar and top with hot sauce, vegetables, noodles, and scallions.

2. When ready to enjoy, pour on some boiling water and cover jar. Let rest for a few minutes before enjoying.

Salmon Salad

This salmon salad is highly nutritious and delicious and requires very little time to make. You can use it on toasts, in sandwiches, as a side, or enjoy it as it is.

Serves: 1

Ready Time: 2 mins

Ingredients:

- 2 (5 to 6 oz) cans of salmon, drained
- 1 medium celery stalk, finely chopped
- 1 tbsp chopped fresh dill
- 3 tbsp finely chopped onion
- ⅓ cup mayonnaise
- Black pepper to taste

Instructions:

1. Add all ingredients to a bowl and mix well.

2. Serve salad.

Garlic Butter Shrimp

Garlic butter shrimp is perfect for topping pasta. It cooks in 4 minutes for a sumptuous treat.

Serves: 1

Ready Time: 4 mins

Ingredients:

- 1 tbsp butter
- 1 garlic clove, minced
- 1 ½ lb. large shrimp, peeled and deveined
- Salt and black pepper to taste
- 1 tbsp chopped fresh thyme
- 2 tbsp chopped fresh parsley
- 1 tbsp chopped fresh cilantro
- ½ lemon, juiced

Instructions:

1. Melt butter in a skillet over medium heat and sauté garlic for 30 seconds.

2. Season shrimp with salt and black pepper and add to skillet. Cook for 1 minute per side.

3. Add thyme, parsley, and cilantro; cook for 1 minute.

4. Drizzle on lemon juice, simmer for 1 minute and turn heat off.

Low-Carb Cheddar Chaffles

Are you on a low-carb diet? If yes, this cheesy chaffle recipe is yours. While this recipe is straightforward, it can accommodate other ingredients like cooked chicken, vegetables, and other types of cheese.

Serves: 1

Ready Time: 2 mins

Ingredients:

- 1 egg
- ½ cup grated cheddar cheese
- 1 tbsp almond flour

Instructions:

1. Preheat a waffle iron.

2. Crack egg into a bowl and whisk. Add cheddar cheese and almond flour and mix well.

3. Pour mixture into waffle iron, cover, and cook for 1 to 2 minutes or until set and golden brown.

4. Transfer chaffle to a plate and serve.

Egg Bagel Sandwich

Make an omelette in the microwave and fill up a bagel with vegetables, cheese, and the eggs you just made. You have a quick and perfect lunch ready.

Serves: 1

Ready Time: 3 mins

Ingredients:

- ¾ cup egg whites
- Salt and black pepper to taste
- 1 bagel, split
- A small handful of spinach
- 1 tbsp garlic cheese
- 2 tomato slices
- 2 to 4 avocado slices

Instructions:

1. Add egg whites to a mug and season with salt and black pepper. Whisk well and microwave for 30 to 60 seconds or until set.

2. Meanwhile, toast bagel in a toaster or skillet for 1 to 2 minutes.

3. Remove egg from microwave and use a spoon to scramble egg.

4. On inner side of both bagel halves, spread garlic cheese.

5. Add spinach to bottom piece, top with egg, tomato, and avocado. Cover with top part of bagel and serve.

Peanut Butter Pie

Peanut butter pie is such a treat. Did you know you could make it in such a little time? Nothing good is compromised here. Enjoy the no-baking-fuss treat.

Serves: 1

Ready Time: 4 mins

Ingredients:

- 3 to 4 graham crackers, crushed
- 1 tbsp melted butter
- 8 oz cream cheese, room temperature
- ¾ cup confectioner's sugar
- ½ cup peanut butter
- 2 tbsp milk of choice
- 8 oz Cool Whip

Instructions:

1. Combine graham crackers and butter in a bowl. Mix well.

2. Spoon and press mixture to fit bottom of small pie pan.

3. In another bowl, combine remaining ingredients and whisk until smooth.

4. Spread mixture evenly on crust.

5. Slice and serve immediately or chill until you're ready to enjoy.

Spicy Avocado Toast

Like we said earlier, toasts allow for amazing toppings like this one. Enjoy the satisfying feel.

Serves: 1

Ready Time: 2 mins

Ingredients:

- 2 bread slices
- ½ avocado, pitted and peeled
- ¼ tsp red chili flakes
- Salt and black pepper to taste
- ¼ tsp fresh lemon juice, optional

Instructions:

1. Toast bread in a toaster or skillet for 1 minute. Transfer to a plate.

2. Mash avocado in a bowl using a fork. Add red chili flakes, salt, black pepper, and lemon juice. Mix well.

3. Spread avocado mixture on toasted bread and enjoy.

Buffalo Chicken Wraps

Who likes some heat? We do! Buffalo chicken is one of our favorites and we love it in this quickly assembled wrap.

Serves: 1

Ready Time: 2 mins

Ingredients:

- 2 cups shredded rotisserie chicken
- 2 tbsp melted butter
- ½ cup buffalo sauce
- 1 cup shredded lettuce
- ¼ cup ranch dressing
- 4 medium flour tortillas
- ½ cup grated Gruyere cheese

Instructions:

1. In a bowl, combine chicken, butter, and buffalo sauce. Mix well.

2. Add lettuce and ranch dressing. Mix well.

3. Warm tortillas in a skillet for 1 to 2 minutes and lay on a clean, flat surface.

4. Spread chicken mixture on center of each tortilla and add cheese. Wrap tortillas over filling and slice in half.

5. Serve.

Million Dollar Dip

Million dollar dip contains everything nice but is ready in almost no time. Enjoy this hearty snack treat.

Serves: 1

Ready Time: 2 mins

Ingredients:

- 5 green onions, chopped
- ½ cup chopped cooked bacon
- 1 cup grated cheddar cheese
- 1½ cups mayonnaise
- ½ cup slivered almonds

Instructions:

1. Add all ingredients to a bowl and mix well.

2. Chill for 2 hours and serve with crackers.

Black Bean Dip

Black bean dip is an intelligent way to use canned black beans. It is a lovely snack pair for chips.

Serves: 1

Ready Time: 2 mins

Ingredients:

- 2 (15 oz) cans black beans, drained and rinsed
- ¾ cup salsa
- 4 garlic cloves, minced
- 2 tsp fresh lime juice
- 1 tsp cumin powder
- 1 tsp water
- Salt to taste
- ¼ cup minced fresh cilantro

Instructions:

1. Combine all ingredients in a food processor except cilantro and process until smooth.

2. Pour dip into a bowl and garnish with cilantro.

3. Serve.

Nut Butter and Berries Oatmeal

Make oatmeal in the microwave for quicker results. After, add some nut butter and berries for a delicious breakfast.

Serves: 2

Ready Time: 2 mins

Ingredients:

- 1 cup steel-cut oats
- ½ to 1 cup milk of choice
- Salt to taste
- 2 tbsp honey or sweetener of choice
- 2 tbsp nut butter
- ½ cup fresh blueberries
- 2 tbsp pomegranate arils
- 2 tbsp toasted nut of choice

Instructions:

1. In a bowl, combine oats, milk, salt, and honey. Mix well.

2. Microwave for 45 seconds to 1 minute or until oatmeal is tender to your liken.

3. Remove from microwave and top with nut butter, blueberries, pomegranate, and nuts.

Turkey and Pesto Panini

Yum, yum, yum! This treat is everything to want during work break lunch. It is aroma-filled, chunky, tasty, and super filling.

Serves: 1

Ready Time: 3 mins

Ingredients:

- 1 loaf ciabatta, split
- ½ cup pesto
- ½ lb. sliced turkey breasts
- 1 large tomato, sliced
- ⅔ cup sliced mozzarella

Instructions:

1. Preheat a panini press.

2. On lower bottom of bread, spread half of pesto and top with turkey, tomato, mozzarella, and remaining pesto. Cover with other piece of bread.

3. Place sandwich in panini press and toast for 1 to 2 minutes.

4. Remove from press, slice in half, and serve.

Conclusion

Do you feel like making your meals now more than getting takeouts? With these quick-cooking recipes, making meals has become easy.

You don't need to fret anymore about long cooking processes. Tag along with cooking technology, grab your favorite recipes and start enjoying.

Cheers!

Biography

Food is like music, and Will knew that when he stepped into the restaurant business. Will loved food, and American classics were always a favorite. He loved the feelings and emotions some of this food invoked in him. Serving unique American dishes was one way to connect his love for music and food on a plate. Customers who would later come into his restaurant could instantly link classic American music stars to the food on their plates. This was a thought well appreciated by the diners.

Even more was that Will researched old and deep-rooted foods in American history, added his spin, and gave the customer a piece of history on the plate.

However, his career did not start in the food industry, but after working as a waiter in a couple of local and renowned All-American restaurants, he went back to culinary school to perfect his skills in plating dishes to aesthetically please the customers as they listened to music from back in the days.

Customers came to his restaurant not because he was a good cook, but to learn the American story behind the meals.

Today, Will has ventured into other food terrains, including serving original cocktails that pair incredibly well with steak and others. He has a restaurant and is making a difference in the lives of his customers.

Thank you

Did you like my book? I pondered it severely before releasing this book. Although the response has been overwhelming, it is always pleasing to see, read or hear a new comment. Thank you for reading this. And I would love to hear your honest opinion about it. Furthermore, many people are searching for a unique book, and your feedback will help me gather the right books for my reading audience.

Thanks!

Will C.

Printed in Great Britain
by Amazon

59551360R00040